Who Was
Harry Houdini?

Who Was
Harry Houdini?

by Tui T. Sutherland
illustrated by John O'Brien

Grosset & Dunlap
An Imprint of Penguin Random House

For Cosmo and George, modern-day magicians—TTS

For Tess—JO'B

GROSSET & DUNLAP
Penguin Young Readers Group
An Imprint of Penguin Random House LLC

Penguin supports copyright. Copyright fuels creativity, encourages diverse voices, promotes free speech, and creates a vibrant culture. Thank you for buying an authorized edition of this book and for complying with copyright laws by not reproducing, scanning, or distributing any part of it in any form without permission. You are supporting writers and allowing Penguin to continue to publish books for every reader.

The publisher does not have any control over and does not assume any responsibility for author or third-party websites or their content.

Text copyright © 2002 by Tui T. Sutherland. Illustrations copyright © 2002 by John O'Brien. Cover illustration copyright © 2002 by Penguin Random House LLC. All rights reserved. Published by Grosset & Dunlap, an imprint of Penguin Random House LLC, 345 Hudson Street, New York, New York 10014. Who HQ™ and all related logos are trademarks owned by Penguin Random House LLC. GROSSET & DUNLAP is a trademark of Penguin Random House LLC. Printed in the USA.

Library of Congress Control Number: 2002004374

ISBN 978-0-448-42686-0   40 39 38 37 36

Contents

Who Was Harry Houdini?

Who was Harry Houdini?

Most people know that he was a famous magician—but did you know that he was also a movie star, a pilot, an acrobat, and a writer?

Harry Houdini (pronounced hoo-DEE-nee) didn't even really like the word "magician." He preferred to call himself an "escape artist." He said he could break out of anything— handcuffs, jail cells, strait- jackets, chains, padlocked boxes, iron cages, anything! People challenged Houdini to escape from all sorts of weird things in all sorts of weird places. And he always succeeded!

Why do people still find him so fascinating? For one thing, a lot of what he did has never been done by anyone else. Many of his tricks are still mysteries. And he told so many fantastic stories about his life that sometimes it's hard to know what was true and what wasn't. We also don't know *why* he did all the crazy and dangerous things that he did. Was it to impress people? Was it because he thought it would make him rich? Or was it because he wanted to be the best in the world at *something*—and he wanted the world to know it? Harry Houdini was certainly a very talented escape artist. More importantly, he was determined. What Houdini wanted, Houdini got. And Houdini wanted attention—lots of it!

In a time before television and movies, Harry Houdini became famous all over the world. *Everybody* knew who he was. He made sure of that! Can you imagine somebody getting famous today without using TV, computers, or movies?

But being famous was very important to Houdini—and his dream came true. Even now, more than 75 years after his death, he is still the most famous magician who ever lived.

Chapter 1
So You Want to Be an American

The year was 1886. A twelve-year-old boy stood on the platform at a train station. He was small but muscular and tough-looking, with dark hair, bright blue-grey eyes, and a frown on his face.

He was not where he meant to be.

He had hopped on a train in Milwaukee, Wisconsin, several hundred miles to the north. His plan was to get to Texas—where he thought the train was going. Along the way, he had sent his mother a postcard.

DEAR MA,
I AM GOING TO GALVESTON TEXAS AND WILL BE HOME IN ABOUT A YEAR.
MY BEST REGARDS TO ALL,
YOUR TRUANT SON,
EHRICH

MRS CECILIA WEISS,
APPLETON,
WISCONSIN

1886

But this was not Texas. The sign on the platform clearly said: "Kansas City, Missouri." Somehow, he had ended up on the wrong train. And now here he was, hundreds of miles and several states away from Texas.

What could he do?

He'd have to make the best of it. After all, he had run away from home so he could earn more money for his family. He planned to run errands, shine shoes, do any jobs he could find. Surely he could do that just as well in Missouri as he could in Texas. So off he went to town, looking for a place to sleep.

In the years to come, this boy would travel a lot farther than Kansas City, Missouri. The nickels and dimes he planned to bring home to his family would one day be hundreds and thousands of dollars. But then, at that point, the young shoeshine boy could never have imagined that one day he'd be a world-famous magician. He had trouble just earning enough money to eat!

Harry Houdini's childhood is full of stories that may or may not be true. He was born on

EASTERN EUROPE IN THE NINETEENTH CENTURY

March 24, 1874, in Budapest, Hungary. His real name was Ehrich Weiss. But during his lifetime, Harry always said his birthday was April 6, because that is what his mother told him. And sometimes he said he was born in America—depending on which reporter he was talking to!

In those days, many people in Europe thought of America as a magical place where all their problems would be solved. Thousands came to the United States from Europe hoping to make a new start in life—and

lots of money, too. Harry's father was one of them.

His name was Mayer Samuel Weiss, and he was a rabbi, a teacher of the Jewish religion. It was hard to be a Jew living in Hungary, where people and laws treated them like second-class citizens and it was difficult to get a job. The Weiss family was very poor. Samuel thought that perhaps he could do better in America. After all, people called it the "land of opportunity." So in 1876, when Ehrich was two years old, Samuel left his wife and sons in Hungary. Although he did not speak a word of English, he set off for America, on the other side of the ocean. It took him two years to save enough money to bring over his family.

Can you imagine what that trip must have been like? First, Harry's mother, Cecilia, and her four sons would have had to get from Hungary to a port city. From there they would board a ship, along

with as many as two thousand other people bound for America. Big ships like

these took anywhere from two weeks to two months to cross the Atlantic Ocean. The passengers had to deal with crowded conditions and limited food. For the rest of his life, Houdini hated traveling by boat.

The Statue of Liberty now stands in New York City's harbor welcoming newcomers to the United States. But it wasn't built yet when Ehrich and the Weiss family arrived. America was a big, strange, new world—and now it was Ehrich's new home.

Unfortunately, life wasn't much easier in the United States. From New York, the Weisses went to live in

Wisconsin, first in a small town called Appleton, and later in the city of Milwaukee. When he was only eight years old, Ehrich started working to help pay the bills. He sold newspapers, shined shoes, and ran errands. At age nine, he also had his first starring act in a backyard circus that he put together with his friends. He called himself "The Prince of the Air" and did stunts on a homemade

trapeze hung from a tree. Later, he made up stories for reporters about this time. He would either say he had been in a real traveling circus as a boy, or that he was already performing his famous escapes at age nine! The truth is he wasn't really interested in magic yet. But he liked

the acrobatics—and the applause.

Not much is known about Ehrich's adventures as a runaway, except that he definitely left home for a while when he was twelve. He may have run away from home more than once, even though he loved his family very much. He always planned to return once he had some money.

Living and traveling on his own made Ehrich resourceful and clever. So when Samuel moved to New York City in 1887, hoping for better luck there, he picked thirteen-year-old

Ehrich to take with him (even though he wasn't the oldest son). Together they raised enough money so that the rest of the family could join them.

But Samuel Weiss died in 1892, leaving his wife with six children to care for. Still, Ehrich was sure he could help out his family. America had not been the land of opportunity for his father, but Ehrich was determined that it would be for him.

Also, before he died, his dad made Ehrich promise something—to always take care of his mother. Ehrich took any promise very seriously, and this one most of all. For the rest of her life, Cecilia Weiss could depend on her "truant son."

There's one story about his childhood that Harry Houdini loved to tell in later years. Whether or not it's true, it certainly sounds like his style. One day in December, while Ehrich was working as a messenger boy, he had an idea. He wrote out a card and stuck it to his hat.

The words on the card were:

Christmas is coming
Turkeys are fat
Please drop a quarter
In the Messenger Boy's hat.

Lots of people laughed and gave him quarters. That night, when he got home, he hid all the quarters in his hair and in his clothes. Then he went to his mother and said, "Shake me! I'm magic!" So she did. Quarters came flying out and went rolling all over the place—like magic!

Then, when he was about sixteen, Ehrich came across a book called *The Memoirs of Robert-Houdin, Ambassador, Author, and Conjuror, Written by Himself.* It was the autobiography of a very famous nineteenth-century French magician. It was full of fantastic stories. Ehrich was hooked.

ROBERT-HOUDIN

Before Jean-Eugène Robert-Houdin (1805–1871), magic shows were performed in outdoor markets or on street corners. Robert-Houdin made magic into an art by doing tricks no one had thought of before. He used new scientific developments in his tricks. (He had started off as a clockmaker!) Like Harry Houdini, Robert-Houdin was very modern. He studied electromagnetism, so he could use powerful magnets to move objects around the stage.

Robert-Houdin was also really clever at promoting himself. His autobiography (published in 1857) was full of exaggerations and wild stories. His skill and style, however, were so successful that, even today, Robert-Houdin is still considered to be "the father of modern magic."

If Robert-Houdin could become so famous through magic, then Ehrich Weiss could, too! But he'd need a catchy stage name. His family called him "Ehrie" (short for Ehrich). That sounded like Harry. And "Houdin" was a name that already made people think of magic. So Harry added an "i" to the end, and tada! Harry Houdini was born.

Chapter 2
So You Want to Be a Magician

Success didn't come "like magic" for Harry. How does someone become a magician, after all? It's not like becoming a doctor or a lawyer. There is no school for magicians. It took Harry years of hard work.

First, of course, a magician has to learn lots of tricks. Harry was always looking for new tricks and illusions, even after he became very famous. He watched other magicians, read books on magic, and wrote everything down in notebooks. He always kept a

notebook by his bed in case he thought of something in the middle of the night.

Being a magician also takes practice, practice, and more practice. Harry practiced his tricks over and over again. He did special exercises to keep his hands and feet flexible and fast. He carried a coin with him and flipped it through his fingers whenever he wasn't performing. Try it—it's harder than it looks!

VANISHING COIN

1   2   3   4

But beyond just learning and practicing, Harry also had to work on selling himself. Even the best magician needs an audience. Harry had to find ways to make people come and see his act. He had to get people's attention.

One of Harry's first magic acts was called "The Brothers Houdini." His younger brother, Theo, was his partner. They did card tricks and mind reading, disappearing acts and illusions.

An illusion is something that seems to have happened but logically couldn't have. For instance, have you ever seen a magician pull a coin out of someone's ear? That's an illusion. Or a magician rips a sheet of paper into bits, then—presto!—it is all back in one piece. Logically, it's not possible for the paper to put itself back together, or for a magician to find a coin in someone's ear. But the trick is done so quickly that it looks real to the people watching.

Harry and Theo did a lot of these kinds of tricks. They did their act anywhere they could find a place to put on their show. And they always set aside money to send home to their mother. One of the most exciting places they performed was in the sideshow at the 1893 World's Fair in Chicago. Harry was just nineteen and Theo was seventeen.

Theo and Harry got along well. Theo was a lot like Harry in some ways—he loved magic too. (He later had a career on his own as a magician.) But there were problems. One night, Theo messed up their best trick. Harry hated mistakes. He insisted on everything being perfect in front of an audience. Theo just couldn't keep up with him.

Harry needed a replacement for Theo— and soon enough, one came along.

In the summer of 1894, the Brothers Houdini performed in the same town as a song- and-dance act called the

Floral Sisters. One of the sisters was a tiny, brown-haired girl called Beatrice Raymond. Like Harry, she had changed her name to go on stage. Her real name was Wilhelmina Rahner. But everyone called her Bess. She was eighteen years old. Harry was twenty.

For Bess and Harry, it was love at first sight. Some stories say they got married only two weeks after they met. According to one of these stories, Bess had to sneak out of her house to go on a date with Harry because she was worried her mother would be mad. Later that evening, she told him she was scared to go home. So he proposed right then and there, and they got married that night! Even if that's not true, they certainly fell in love and got married quickly. It's also true that Bess's mother wasn't happy about it. Bess's family was Catholic. Harry was Jewish, the son of a rabbi. But Harry's mother didn't mind. She thought Bess was just wonderful. And so did Harry.

Bess was more than a perfect wife; she was an ideal stage partner, too. Already used to performing, she was happy to sing and dance between Harry's acts, and she would always

announce him with great style. She also learned the tricks quickly, so she could help him with everything.

Bess was tiny—only five feet tall! That made even Harry look big, and he was only about 5'5" or 5'6". Her size also meant she could slip in and out of tight places, which was very useful for escape tricks.

Even later on, when Harry did solo shows, Bess traveled with him everywhere. She managed his schedule, kept track of his performances, and made sure he remembered to change his shirt every day. Harry said she was the reason for his fame: "She brought me luck and it has been with me ever since. I never had any before I married her." Harry and Bess were together until the day he died.

In the 1890s, Harry, with help from Bess, performed in large halls called dime museums. For ten cents people could enter and watch strange and bizarre acts—sword-swallowers, performing monkeys, jugglers. Houdini would do his Metamorphosis trick.

A small, serious-looking young man in a shabby tuxedo, Houdini stood on a box, waving to the crowds. With him was Bess, wearing woolen tights and a puffy white blouse.

First Harry would pick a few people out from the audience—a "committee" to examine the "apparatus". The apparatus was a tall cabinet with a trunk inside. The trunk was big enough to hold a person. The committee had to inspect the trunk. They knocked on all its sides. They looked inside. Finally they would announce that everything seemed to be normal—no hidden doors or anything.

Then Harry gave the committee a large black bag and some heavy tape. Following his instructions, they tied his hands together, helped him into the bag, and taped the bag shut as tightly as they could. Then the bag with Harry inside was put in the trunk. The trunk was also locked, tied securely with heavy ropes, and placed inside the cabinet.

Once this was all done, Bess closed the curtain in front of the cabinet.

"Now, ladies and gentlemen," she would say, pausing dramatically, "I shall clap my hands three times, and on my last clap I ask you to watch . . . closely . . ." As she clapped, she stepped behind the curtain. Not three seconds later, the curtain swept open. And who was standing there before the audience? Harry Houdini! But what happened to Bess?

Harry turned to the trunk, which was still sealed shut. With the help of the committee, he untied and unlocked the trunk to reveal the bag. And when they opened the bag—there was Bess, tied up the same way Harry had been!

This was the same trick that Theo had messed up once before. But Bess was smaller.

METAMORPHOSIS TRICK

The apparatus is inspected by the committee.

Harry is placed in a sack and trunk as attendants tie his hands and close the sack.

The trunk is tied with strong rope and locked with a heavy chain. The trunk is placed in the cabinet.

Bess closes the curtain in front of the cabinet, addresses the audience, claps three times, and steps behind the curtain.

When the curtain is opened, Harry is standing next to the trunk.

He then opens the trunk and sack to reveal Bess.

HOW IT'S DONE

Harry unties his hands, cuts through the bottom of the sack with a hidden knife, and crawls out a sliding panel on the back of the trunk. Bess then crawls through the panel and into the sack, replacing Harry.

And she was so quick that she could do it in no time at all, exactly the way Harry wanted. The change—or "metamorphosis"—happened so fast, it looked like real magic!

Chapter 3
So You Want to Be Famous

Metamorphosis was an amazing illusion, but it wasn't enough to make "The Houdinis" as famous as Harry wanted to be. The show needed to add something new and dramatic.

Harry tried a lot of different things. With Bess, he did mind-reading acts, circus acrobatics, and even faked "talking to the dead" a few times. How did he talk to the dead? Research and cleverness. When they got to a new town, Harry read local newspapers. He'd go to the graveyard to see who had just died. He listened to people tell stories about friends. Then, on stage, he would use this information to make people think he was really talking to ghosts. It was very believable to the audience. Houdini gave up "talking to the dead" after only a few performances, however. He didn't like the idea of tricking people this way. It was not the same as "magic" where the audience knew that some illusion or trick had to be involved.

Luckily, Harry finally did find something unique to make him famous: escapes. Other magicians had used handcuffs in their acts before Houdini, but he was the first who made it the main attraction of his show. He was also the first person to try escaping from a straitjacket in front of an audience.

Straitjackets are complicated coats with straps and buckles. They are used to keep someone violent from hurting himself or others. A person in a straitjacket can't use their arms and

FRONT   BACK

Expand chest and shoulders as jacket is being tightened

Deflate chest and shoulders and work arms up and over the head

With the arms loose you can now work open the buckles on back of jacket until free

hands at all. Harry thought that he could get out of one. After a lot of practice and effort, he really could. And it looked impressive on stage! He decided not to hide behind a curtain for this part of the show, because it wasn't a trick at all. It just took a lot of skill and effort (and practice). Even after watching him do it, the audience couldn't really explain how it was done—and certainly no one else could do it!

Harry also came up with a really terrific way to promote his act. Whenever he and Bess arrived in a new town, he'd go straight to the local police station.

"I am Harry Houdini, King of Handcuffs!" he would announce. "Lock me up, tie me up, put any and all of your handcuffs on me. I guarantee you I will escape in no time at all."

The police officers usually laughed at him. Who did this short guy with the big mouth think he was? They'd never heard of any "Harry Houdini." Everybody figured that magicians used trick handcuffs. Nobody could escape from real handcuffs. They were so sure of this that they let Harry bring reporters from the local paper to watch. The police officers would search Harry for tools. (Sometimes they even insisted he do his trick naked—so they could be sure he wasn't hiding any keys in his clothing.) Then they would tie him up, snap a few pairs of handcuffs on his hands and feet,

and leave him alone in a room, or lock him in one of their jail cells.

"We'll come back and let you out in a little while," the policemen joked. Then they'd sit in the next room to talk about this crazy show-off. Imagine their surprise a couple of minutes later. In walked Harry, holding the handcuffs up in one hand. Sometimes he was able to free himself in less than a minute.

The policemen and the news reporters were amazed. They couldn't figure out how he had done it. Harry didn't get paid for these stunts, but that didn't matter because of all the stories in the newspapers. The attention made people come to his show. They wanted to see the magician who could trick their own policemen.

The trouble was that this only worked in one town at a time. He could do this in a small city in Missouri, and be a big hit for one night. But as soon as he moved on to the next place, he'd be Mr. Nobody again, and he'd have to start all over. Remember, there was no television or Internet. It was hard to spread news around the country, especially about one small magic act.

By 1899, Harry and Bess had been on the road together for five long years. Harry was becoming discouraged. He started offering to sell his magic secrets. He even thought of quitting the magic business altogether. Then, just in the nick of time, Harry was discovered.

A man saw the Houdinis performing one night. He said to Harry, "Hey, that's quite a show you've got there. Tell you

what—leave out the card tricks and paper-tearing illusions. Just give me twenty minutes of escapes, including 'Metamorphosis,' and I'll make you famous."

So who was this man? He was Martin Beck, in charge of the famous Orpheum Circuit. The Orpheum Circuit was a nationwide chain of theaters—or "vaudeville houses."

Vaudeville houses were a lot classier than dime museums. Each night there was a show with many different acts: singers, dancers, acrobats, comedians, and so on. Martin saw that Harry's act would be perfect for vaudeville. It was new, it was different, and it was exciting. He thought Harry could be a huge success. Of course, Harry had always thought so, too.

They were right. Almost overnight, Harry became a sensation. He finally had time to focus on what he was best at—escapes. By the end of 1899, he was earning over $100 a week, which was a lot of money back then. Best of all, he was getting the attention he had always dreamed of.

Now, not only was Harry ready for the world, but the world was ready for him.

Chapter 4
So You Want to Be a Star

After fourteen months, the stages of the Orpheum Circuit theaters began to seem small to Harry. It was no longer enough for him to be a success in America. To be a real star, Harry Houdini had to conquer Europe.

In May of 1900, twenty-two years after coming to America, he crossed the Atlantic again, this time in the other direction, with Bess and their dog, Charlie. It was still a long trip (the faster ships took two 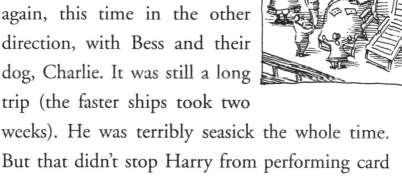 weeks). He was terribly seasick the whole time. But that didn't stop Harry from performing card tricks for the other passengers.

Harry began his European tour in England. Of course, when Harry and Bess first arrived, nobody had ever heard of Harry Houdini. He had to start selling himself all over again. But this

time, it didn't take long. The "King of Handcuffs" baffled London's top police force, Scotland Yard, by escaping from their handcuffs. The news of this feat got Houdini into London's top theater, the Alhambra.

The Alhambra was the most impressive stage Harry had ever performed on. It looked more like an opera house than a vaudeville hall. The audiences were more elegant and reserved. In America, Harry had received some bad reviews because of mistakes in grammar and shabby costumes. Now he appeared every night in a formal tuxedo with a white bow tie. He polished his speech so he sounded more dignified, but still dramatic. And he kept practicing and thinking of new tricks to add to his act.

All of it worked. Audiences loved Houdini. Harry performed at the Alhambra for all of July and August, and then came back at Christmas, too. Originally, the plan had been for Harry to do a few shows in Europe and then return to America. As it turned out, Harry and Bess ended up staying in Europe for five years.

The Houdinis toured many countries in Europe. Everywhere they went, Harry tried to learn some of the language, so he could speak it during his show. This was easiest in Germany, because he had grown up speaking German with his parents. German audiences adored him, and he was a huge success there. It was dangerous, though. The German police sometimes locked up entertainers for "deceiving the public." Performers had to have their act approved by the police.

Houdini had to "audition" in front of three hundred policemen. They provided all the locks and searched Harry for keys beforehand. To protect the secrecy of his act, they let him perform it under a blanket. Of course, he escaped easily—in just six minutes! Since the police couldn't explain how he did it, they let him go on with his show.

Harry's hardest test came in a town called Blackburn, in England. At the time, Harry was offering twenty-five British pounds—a lot of money—to anyone whose cuffs he couldn't escape from. On October 24, 1902, in the middle of his act, a man suddenly walked up on stage. His name was William Hodgson, and he wanted to take Harry up on his bet. Right away Harry was suspicious of Hodgson's handcuffs. They looked like they had been damaged, maybe even broken—

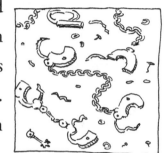

making them harder to unlock. But Hodgson teased him, saying Houdini was afraid to take a real challenge. Harry Houdini would never stand for that.

Hodgson was a physical fitness expert who had carefully studied the human body and how all the muscles work. He knew exactly how to tie a man up so that he would not be able to move at

all. And this is what he did to Houdini, using chains and six pairs of handcuffs. People watching were worried that Harry's circulation would be cut off completely, or that Hodgson might break Harry's bones twisting his arms around so roughly. But the hardest part for Harry was that his escape skills depended on his strength and flexibility. If he couldn't move a muscle, those skills couldn't help him.

The audience waited for a terrifying hour and a half while Houdini struggled behind the curtain. At one point, Harry asked for his wrists to be unlocked just for a minute, because his hands had gone numb and he couldn't feel them anymore. Hodgson refused, saying "If you are beaten, just give in." Harry Houdini, beaten? Impossible! Back behind the curtain he went.

Just after midnight, suddenly the curtain was thrown back. There was Harry, triumphantly flinging the last of the handcuffs down on the stage. One reporter later said he looked "as though some tiger had  clawed him." He was bleeding and bruised all over, but he was free. The crowd went totally crazy.

Another incident in England drew headlines. A newspaper called the *London Daily Illustrated Mirror* challenged Houdini to escape from a single pair of "the most difficult handcuffs ever invented." How could Harry say no?

The Mirror Cuffs, as they were called, were made by a man in Birmingham, England, who claimed it had taken five years to make them. As Houdini knew from years of studying locksmiths, most locks involve simple mechanisms. They can be undone using a few basic keys or even a sharp tap in the right place. But these handcuffs were several thousand times more complicated. Only one key in the world could unlock them—and that key belonged to the man who made them.

For days before the show, newspapers ran stories about the Mirror Cuffs and the challenge. Harry loved it; the more attention he got, the better. Finally, the big night came. Harry appeared onstage to a standing ovation. As usual, a committee from the audience was chosen to make sure everything was fair. The *Mirror* reporter snapped the cuffs onto Harry's wrists, and the locksmith turned the key six times.

Harry announced, "I am now locked up in handcuffs that have taken a British mechanic five years to make. I do not know whether I am going to get out of it or not, but I can assure you I am going to do my best."

Harry disappeared behind a curtain on stage. For a long time, the audience saw nothing but the curtain moving every now and then.

This was another interesting thing about Harry's act. Most of it took place behind a curtain, with the audience waiting for something to happen. Can you imagine going to a show today and spending most of the time staring at a curtain? Audiences were a lot more patient back then. And Harry was so magnetic and dazzling on stage that even the few minutes he did appear made the whole rest of the show worth it. Besides, there was always the question: Would he be able to escape? Or—would he fail?

After several minutes with the Mirror Cuffs, Harry came out from behind the curtain, looking exhausted. Had he escaped? No! He wanted a cushion, to rest his knees on. Then he went back.

Soon he stepped out again. But wait—he was still handcuffed! This time he asked for the handcuffs to be unlocked for a minute, so that he could take off his coat. The *Mirror* representative said no. Watching the handcuffs being unlocked might give Harry clues about how to escape from them. The cuffs would stay on until Harry admitted defeat.

Admit defeat? Harry Houdini? Never! Right onstage, using his teeth and twisting his arms around, Harry managed to get a small

penknife from his jacket pocket. Dramatically, he flipped his coat over his head and, with the knife in his teeth, slashed at his coat until it fell to the floor in pieces. He tossed his head proudly, turned, and disappeared behind the curtain again.

Only ten minutes later—Harry leapt out, holding the Mirror Cuffs high over his head. He had done it. The King of Handcuffs had triumphed! The crowd went wild, and the story stayed in the newspapers for days. It had taken five years to make the handcuffs. But it had taken Houdini only one hour to escape from them.

Harry had many more adventures in Europe. In Paris, he went and visited the grave of his hero, Jean Eugène Robert-

Houdin. In fact, he visited the graves of lots of famous magicians and always left big wreaths of flowers for them. He also visited many well-known, retired magicians. Some of them even shared their secrets with him, impressed by his success and charm.

Perhaps the least welcoming country Harry traveled to was Russia. As a Jew, he wasn't allowed in on his own passport. The Houdinis had to use Bess's passport and papers, because she was a Roman Catholic. Harry found the country very cold and frightening.

"If any country ever was police-ruled, why that country is Russia," he wrote. It also made him realize more than anywhere else how many people hated Jews. This kind of prejudice, anti-Semitism, was part of the reason his family had left Europe so many years before.

For the most part, however, Harry loved Europe. Even after months in one city, he could still sell out shows every night. In America, he would have been traveling to a new place every week or so. He was also making an astonishing amount of money in Europe. Still, Harry really missed his mother. He sent money to her all the time and visited her twice between 1900 and 1905. But he wanted to be closer to her. And he didn't want America to forget about him. So, in 1905, America saw the return of Harry Houdini— huge international star.

Chapter 5
So You Want to Be Amazing

From then on, there was no stopping Harry Houdini. He went all over America, and all over the world. He challenged anyone to lock him into something he couldn't get out of. And he escaped from some pretty strange things—including a giant football! He also added a new element to his show: water.

In 1908, Houdini debuted an entirely new trick—one that he said was "the best I have ever invented!" The audience in the theater was on the edge of their seats. Harry had started off the show with some of his standard acts—illusions, Metamorphosis, handcuff escapes. Now he turned and walked downstage toward the audience. Stepping over the footlights at the bottom of the stage, he leaned forward as if he was about to leap into the first row of seats, and spread his arms wide.

"LADIES AND GENTLEMEN!" Harry boomed. His voice carried to the back row. This wasn't the shabbily dressed, quiet boy of the dime museum days. His personality electrified the theater. "Now, for the first time ever, here today I introduce to you my latest and greatest escape, the most amazing act ever seen on an American stage!"

With a flourish, Harry revealed a giant iron milk can, large enough for a small person to squeeze into. He thumped it on all sides to show

how sturdy it was. Then he went offstage to change into a bathing suit, while his assistants filled the can to the brim with water.

Finally, Harry climbed into the can. "As I am submerged in water," he said to the audience, "try timing yourselves, too, to see how long you can hold your breath." He also pointed to one of his assistants, holding a large axe. "In case something goes terribly wrong, do not fear. My loyal assistant will smash open the can and free me . . . let's just hope it's in time!"

With a grin, Houdini allowed himself to be handcuffed and squeezed into the can. His assistants locked down the steel cover with massive padlocks. In later versions of this escape, Harry would also invite audience members to bring their own padlocks, to close the cover even more securely.

A curtain was drawn in front of the can. People in the audience held their breath. The

seconds passed . . . a whole minute went by. By this point, most of the people watching were gasping for air. It is very dangerous to hold your breath for that long. And still there was no sign of Houdini. Another minute passed, then another. The audience was frantic. What if Houdini had drowned? How would anyone know? "Let him out!" they started calling. "Smash open the can, he's drowning!"

Then suddenly, Harry swept aside the curtain and bowed. He was dripping wet and gasping for breath, but alive and free. And the can stood there, still padlocked securely.

It was a sensational trick. The audience couldn't get enough of it. And Harry liked playing with people's minds, too, to make the escape seem more dramatic. Sometimes he would get out of the can in a couple of minutes, and then wait behind the curtain for up to half an hour, letting the tension build. Once everyone was terrified that the trick hadn't worked, and that Houdini was dead, then he'd make his dramatic entrance to thunderous applause.

Harry had always been a good swimmer and comfortable in the water. He also practiced a lot for this very dangerous trick. He'd fill a bathtub with water and have Bess time him to see how long he could stay under. Or he'd make the water freezing cold and see how long he could stand it. This was useful for another new and even more dangerous trick—his river escapes.

For this act, Harry would usually start on a bridge, surrounded by thousands of spectators

(and reporters, of course!). He would strip down to a bathing suit or long underwear and allow policemen to lock him into two or more pairs of handcuffs. Then he'd climb up on the railing, wave, shout farewell to the crowd, and leap off the bridge into the freezing water. Splash! The audience hung over the railing, searching the water. Sometimes Houdini would pop right back up, holding the handcuffs triumphantly over his head. Or sometimes he would stay underwater longer, making everybody wait. A couple of times, he even swam off underwater to someplace where he could hide.

Harry always said that these were his most dangerous escapes. He warned other people not to try them. But people did anyway, and some of them died. Not only was the water dangerously cold, but sometimes the current would pull Houdini away from the boat where his assistants were waiting to help him out. Once he got trapped under ice, after the current swept him away from the hole he'd jumped through.

Houdini kept coming up with new and more dangerous twists for his underwater escapes. Sometimes he'd attach large, heavy objects to his handcuffs, so he'd get pulled down to the bottom of the water faster. Or sometimes after being tied up, he'd also be nailed inside a wooden box, which was then dropped in the river.

He did bridge jumps in cities all over the U.S., from Rochester, New York, to Boston, Massachusetts, to New Orleans, Louisiana. There was no way to charge money for these kinds of stunts, but Harry didn't mind. As with his earlier police challenges, he was excited by the fame and attention. It wasn't hard to advertise himself now. Tens of thousands of people would come out to see one of his jumps.

There was nothing Houdini liked better than a big crowd!

Chapter 6
So You Want to Be a Pilot

Harry loved being famous. He liked being the best. He also liked being *first*.

Airplanes came into use during Harry's lifetime. He was already almost thirty years old when the Wright Brothers made history in 1903 by flying the first plane at Kitty Hawk, North Carolina. Planes were dangerous, unpredictable machines, with few of the safety features they have now. Harry hated boats, and he couldn't even drive.

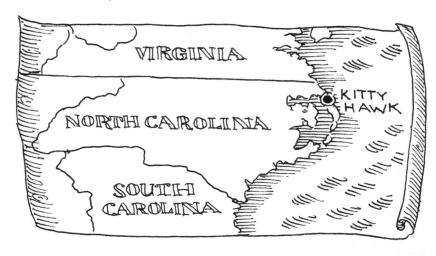

THE WRIGHT BROTHERS

WILBUR 1867–1912   ORVILLE 1871–1948

Almost five hundred years ago, Leonardo da Vinci tried to design machines that would let people fly. But nobody built a successful one until December 17, 1903, when two brothers from Ohio finally took to the skies in a small plane they built themselves.

Orville and Wilbur Wright owned a bicycle shop, and working on bicycles taught them how important balance is—both for riding a bike and flying a plane. They realized that it would take a lot of research to design an airplane, so they decided to do their own studies and calculations. Although neither had graduated from high school, they taught themselves everything they needed to know about flight, wind, physics—anything that would be useful. They even built their own engine so that it would be exactly the right size and weight for their plane.

And finally, on that cold December day in Kitty Hawk, North Carolina, their plane took off. The first flight lasted only twelve seconds, but it was a historical turning point that forever changed the world.

But the very first time Harry saw a plane, he knew he had to learn to fly. Not only that: he had to be a part of aviation history.

The Wright Brothers' first flight lasted only about twelve seconds. By 1909, not even six years later, someone had already flown across the English Channel between England and France. Someone had been the first to fly at night, the first to fly with passengers, the first to fly in France, in Germany, in Italy. It was getting hard to find something new and historical to do, even for an experienced pilot. And Harry was a beginner. Yet he still was determined to make his mark as an airplane pilot. So he came up with a plan.

In January of 1910, Harry and Bess found themselves on board a massive steamship. They would be on this boat for over a month, despite Harry's seasickness. What convinced him to take an ocean voyage this long? Where were they going?

Australia.

Thousands of miles from anywhere Harry had been before, Australia was still a new, developing land. Hardly any performer of his fame was willing to make the long trip to the Southern continent. But Australia was also one place where nobody had flown a plane yet. Harry could be the first.

Harry bought himself a plane called a Voisin. He hired a mechanic and packed everything onto the steamship with him. All through the month-long journey, no matter how sick he felt, Harry could think about his plane stowed safely below.

Once in Australia, Harry had to fit in flying time around his demanding performance schedule. And there were always problems. Planes were still fragile machines, so he couldn't try flying when it was very windy, or foggy, or if it rained too much. Harry had to wait more than a month before he and his plane actually got off the ground.

On the morning of March 18, 1910, a group of reporters watched nervously as Harry drove the plane slowly around the field. After a few short hops into the air to make sure everything was in order, Harry pointed the plane at the far end of the field. His whole body was tense and shaking. But he was determined. He accelerated forward . . . going faster . . . and faster . . . until up into the air he went!

Official records say that this, the first real flight in Australia, lasted about three and a half minutes, and the plane rose as high as one hundred feet in the air. That was enough to make the record books, and enough for Harry. Although he flew a few more times in Australia, his interest died. Once he and Bess left Australia, he never

flew again. "I had had my adventure in the air," was how Harry explained it.

A few years later, Harry Houdini got to meet the famous Orville Wright. It turned out that Orville knew more about Harry's flying experience than about Houdini's magic!

Chapter 7
So You Want to Be a Movie Star

Soon enough, Harry found something else new to capture his interest. The early 1900s introduced the first movies to be seen in theaters. Harry was twenty-one when the first movie was shown on a big screen in a theater in Paris. These early movies were black and white, and silent, with music provided by live orchestras. The movies were very short and the action looked very jumpy. Still, people all over the world were fascinated by them. Of course, Harry never missed an opportunity to make himself more famous. What could be more perfect than a movie career?

Harry's first movie was called *The Master Mystery*. It opened in theaters in 1919. It was a serial. That meant it was shown in weekly

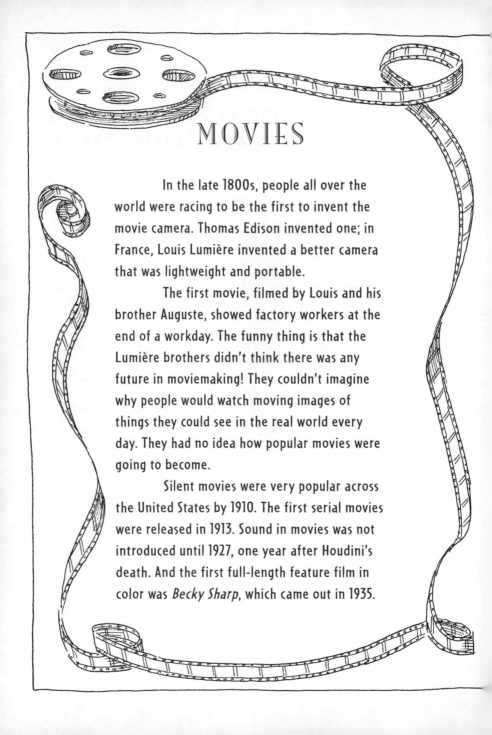

MOVIES

In the late 1800s, people all over the world were racing to be the first to invent the movie camera. Thomas Edison invented one; in France, Louis Lumière invented a better camera that was lightweight and portable.

The first movie, filmed by Louis and his brother Auguste, showed factory workers at the end of a workday. The funny thing is that the Lumière brothers didn't think there was any future in moviemaking! They couldn't imagine why people would watch moving images of things they could see in the real world every day. They had no idea how popular movies were going to become.

Silent movies were very popular across the United States by 1910. The first serial movies were released in 1913. Sound in movies was not introduced until 1927, one year after Houdini's death. And the first full-length feature film in color was *Becky Sharp*, which came out in 1935.

installments, instead of all at once—more like a television show than a movie. In serials, each week's episode ended with a thrilling cliffhanger; for example, with the heroine tied to the tracks in front of an oncoming train. The audience would have to come back a week later to find out whether the star escaped or not—and how.

It's almost as if this kind of moviemaking was designed with Harry Houdini in mind. His whole career was about getting into situations that seemed impossible to escape from. Each episode of *The Master Mystery* ended with Harry trapped and in terrible danger. Then the next one began with his escape, so he could go after "the bad guys." Sounds like a great TV show, doesn't it? Now audiences could see some of Houdini's famous escapes on screen.

Careful not to give away his secrets, the movie did show how much skill and strength were involved in the escapes. For instance, in one scene

Harry's hands were chained to a wall. So he used his toes like fingers—reaching for a ring of keys, picking out the right key, and unlocking the door to his cell.

The plot of the movie was very complicated, but exciting. Harry played an undercover agent for the government, and the villain was a robot. Even though it was obvious that there was a human inside the robot outfit, it was still a new and interesting twist for a movie. *The Master Mystery* featured the first robot villain in movie history.

The Master Mystery was an international hit. People in places like India and Japan saw Harry Houdini for the first time. Of course, most of the people who saw the movie already knew who he was. By this point, Houdini didn't really need a movie to increase his fame. But he loved the attention, and people loved watching him. Harry was ready to make more movies.

Houdini starred in four more films over the next four years. But each one made less and less money. After *The Master Mystery*, Houdini switched to starring in full-length feature films, not serials. Perhaps that was part of the problem—audiences weren't left in the same state of suspense week after week. *The Grim Game, Terror Island, The Man From Beyond,* and *Haldane of the Secret Service* all got terrible reviews. Most critics agreed: Harry was a terrific escape artist who couldn't act at all.

The biggest problem, though, was that there was no way for the audience to tell the real Houdini

escapes from escapes created by camera tricks. Although Harry did most of his own stunts, moviegoers knew how easy it was to fake "danger" on screen. The nature of Harry's act made it much more thrilling when it was seen live.

Still, Harry got to be a movie star, and he even got a star on the Hollywood Walk of Fame.

Chapter 8
So You Want to Be an Illusionist

As Harry got older, some of his escapes became harder for him to perform. First he cut out handcuff tricks from his act; other performers were copying those tricks anyway. Then he started replacing his dangerous escapes with big, remarkable illusions.

Most magicians, including Harry, start their careers with illusions. A classic example is pulling a rabbit out of a hat. Harry wanted to take illusions to a whole new level. And he did.

One of his new illusions used screens and an actual brick wall. Harry would have a team of bricklayers build a wall down the center of the stage, right in front of the audience. The stage floor was covered with a large sheet, pinned

BRICK WALL TRICK

A sheet is laid on the stage floor and a brick wall is built on a wheeled frame.

Audience volunteers inspect the wall as assistants place screens on both sides of the wall.

Houdini moves behind the screen on one side of the wall and then emerges from the other side.

THE TRICK

Sheet ←

Stage **Trap door** →

An assistant releases a trap door below the stage, allowing the sheet to sag just enough for Houdini to crawl beneath the wall.

underneath the wall, and Harry would ask volunteers to come up and stand around the edges of the sheet. Then he would stand on one side of the wall, and his assistants would put a screen around him. They would put another screen on the other side of the wall. Then everyone would stand back and wait.

Harry, waving his hand over the top of the screen, would call, "You see, I am over here!" Then the hand would disappear, his assistants would take away the screen, and—no Harry. A moment later, Harry would walk out from behind the screen—on the other side of the wall.

How did he do it? The people onstage could see that he hadn't walked around the back. The audience had seen the wall being built, so they knew there wasn't a secret door or way through it. And surely the sheet on the stage floor guaranteed that he hadn't somehow gone under the wall.

Well, not exactly. In actual fact, that's just

what he did. There was a trapdoor in the stage just under the wall. Once everything was in place, one of his assistants would hide under the stage and open the trapdoor. There was just enough room for Harry to squeeze between the bottom of the wall and the sheet. Everyone standing on the sheet kept it from moving while Harry squeezed through. They thought they were preventing Houdini from tricking them. Instead, they were actually helping him.

Another of Harry's great illusions cannot be explained so easily. A lot of magicians make things "disappear"—a rabbit, a coin, even a person. But Harry wanted to perform the biggest disappearing act in the whole world. That's how he came up with his next trick: The Vanishing Elephant.

Harry performed this illusion only in the biggest theaters where there was room on stage for an elephant. He would start out by introducing his elephant who was named Jenny. Then Harry's

VANISHING ELEPHANT

Harry leads Jenny the elephant to a large cabinet on the stage.

Jenny enters the cabinet through the curtains and is out of the audience's view.

The cabinet is folded open to reveal that Jenny has vanished.

THE TRICK

Through spring doors at the rear of the cabinet, Jenny enters a hidden cage on wheels, where Jenny is trained to find her favorite foods.

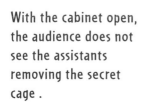

With the cabinet open, the audience does not see the assistants removing the secret cage.

assistants would roll in a very large box on wheels, large enough to hold Jenny. Harry would walk around the box, opening the doors on all sides, so the audience could see that there were no hidden sections at the back. Harry would lead Jenny inside and close all the doors.

A few seconds later, Harry would sweep open the doors again. Jenny was gone. Once again, he'd walk around the box and open all the doors. She had vanished!

Audiences were amazed. How did he do it? The trick was in the construction of the box. But as far as the audience could tell, Harry had made an elephant disappear.

Chapter 9
So You Want to Be a Hero

The first time Harry performed the Vanishing Elephant trick was on January 1, 1918, in a giant building called the Hippodrome, in New York City. It was part of a spectacular magic show that Harry put on to raise money for the families of American soldiers killed in World War I. This was something that Harry cared about a lot, so it was important to him to do something new and amazing.

World War I broke out in Europe in 1914, while Harry was on tour in America. For a long time, the United States stayed out of the war. Harry cancelled his shows in Germany. He also started telling reporters stories that made him sound more American. That was because of all the

WORLD WAR I

Begun on June 28, 1914, the First World War pitted Russia, Britain, Italy and France against Germany, Austria, and what is now Turkey. It was the first "modern" war, with frightening new weapons like machine guns and tanks. Both sides were powerful and well-armed. And neither side was willing to give in. The war dragged on for more than four years; about ten million people died.

When the war started, President Woodrow Wilson was determined to keep the United States out of it. He told people to remain neutral, and he tried to maintain trading and diplomatic relations with both sides. But on May 7, 1915, a German submarine attacked the British ship *Lusitania*. One hundred and twenty-eight Americans were killed. Then in early 1917, German submarines started sinking all ships bound for Britain, including American ones. Soon President Wilson, and the United States, had no choice but to join the war. American troops, supplies, and weapons helped turn the tide of the war, and finally, in November 1918, the Germans surrendered and peace was reached.

anti-German feeling in the country. Harry did not want to be associated with the enemy.

Harry kept touring and performing as usual. But it was a sad time, personally, for Harry. On July 17, 1913, he suffered "a shock from which I do not think recovery is possible." His mother, Cecilia Weiss, died.

All his life, Harry had kept his promise to his father. He always sent money home to his mother and took care of her. She lived with Harry and Bess in New York City till her dying day. Often Harry had brought Cecilia along to Europe to see him perform. He always said that his mother and Bess were his two sweethearts.

Just as Harry had always feared, Cecilia died while he was away in Europe. As soon as he heard the news, he cancelled the rest of the tour (including a performance

for the king of Sweden) and rushed home for the funeral. For the rest of his life he continued to mourn her death. Some people he met said it was all he could talk about. For the next few years, he was sad and unfocused, even though he kept on performing.

Luckily for Harry, Bess was always at his side. She supported Harry through everything. Even when he was perfecting his most dangerous stunts, she never doubted that he would come back to her safe and sound. Sometimes he worried more than she did. Once, right before a bridge jump, he handed a friend a piece of paper that just said "I leave everything to Bess." He wanted to make sure she would be provided for if something should happen to him.

In April 1917, the United States decided to join the war in Europe. Harry signed up for military service that same month. He was determined to help however he could.

Unfortunately, Harry, now forty-three, was too old to join the army, even though he was in better shape than many younger men. So Harry found other ways to help. Millions of people were willing to pay money to see Harry perform— so why not give some of that money to the war effort?

Harry did shows all across the United States to raise money for American troops. Not only that, he also performed for thousands of soldiers. He did shows for the wounded in army camps. He even taught classes for soldiers before they went off to war, showing them how to escape from German

handcuffs and locks. Harry had always guarded his secrets carefully; now he revealed some of them. It was worth it if he could help America win.

"It is not a question of 'will we win' or 'will we lose,'" he wrote. "WE MUST WIN, and that is all there is to it." The Hippodrome benefit alone (where he introduced the Vanishing Elephant) raised nearly ten thousand dollars for families of American soldiers.

All his life Houdini devoted time to what he called "Good Works." These included donating money to hospitals and orphanages, where he also performed for free. Children adored him, and he especially loved doing his show for them.

It always made Harry sad that he and Bess never had children. It was the one thing missing from their marriage. He was jealous of his brother, Theo, who had sons. But Bess and Harry were happy together anyway. For them, pets became like children. Their dog, Charlie, traveled with them for eight years.

Harry and Bess also had many friends, although he was too busy to have much of a social life. He loved meeting other famous people—especially ones who knew who he was. On one boat trip between Europe and America, he astonished former president Teddy Roosevelt with some of his tricks. For the rest of his life, Harry treasured the photograph he had of the two of them together.

HARRY AND TEDDY

CHARLIE AND HARRY

There are also photographs of Houdini with Charlie Chaplin and Buster Keaton, two of the greatest comic stars of the silent screen. And Houdini became good friends with Jack London, author of *The Call of the Wild* and *White Fang*. He also met Sir Arthur Conan Doyle, the man who created Sherlock Holmes. But this friendship ended less happily for Harry Houdini.

HARRY AND JACK

Chapter 10
So You Want to Be a Detective

Sir Arthur Conan Doyle was an English writer, famous for his bestselling mysteries about the great detective Sherlock Holmes. Holmes was brilliant and observant—he could tell a hundred things about a man just by looking at and listening to him. Sherlock Holmes used logic to solve mysteries, like putting together the pieces of a complicated puzzle. Nobody could fool him. But his creator, Sir Arthur Conan Doyle, was not much like his famous sharp-eyed, suspicious hero.

When Houdini and Conan Doyle met, Sir Arthur had recently become interested in a new movement called "Spiritualism." Spiritualism was very popular after World War I, in the 1920s. Spiritualists claimed to communicate with ghosts and spirits of the dead. After the war, many people wanted to believe—needed to believe—they could contact their lost loved ones.

At a séance, people calling themselves mediums would gather a group around a table and try to communicate with the dead. Mediums used a lot of mysterious phenomena to show that ghosts were really present . . . floating objects, strange knocks on the table, instruments that played themselves.

SIR ARTHUR CONAN DOYLE

According to Sir Arthur, Spiritualism was "absolutely the most important development in the whole history of the human race." Harry didn't believe a word of it. He knew how talking to the dead worked; it had been a part of his

SPIRITUALISM

Spiritualism became very popular in the United States in the late 1800s. Two sisters, Margaret and Catherine Fox, claimed that they could hear a ghost in their house. The sisters claimed that they could interpret the ghost's rapping noises that were actually messages from the spirit world. Their sessions with the ghost became performances that people could attend. Soon the girls started touring all across the country, "speaking" with a number of other spirits.

The popularity of the Fox act attracted thousands of people who flocked to what they believed was a new religious movement—Spiritualism. However, Spiritualism suffered a blow in 1888 when Margaret Fox publicly admitted that she and her sister were frauds. They had made the rapping sounds by cracking their toes. She wanted people to know it was all tricks and lies.

But a lot of people refused to believe that Spiritualism was fake. One of these was Sir Arthur Conan Doyle, who insisted that Harry Houdini really had supernatural powers.

own show when he was very young. But he stopped doing it, because it was wrong to trick people. He was convinced that all these new mediums were fakes, too.

Sir Arthur's belief in Spiritualism appalled Harry. How could such a smart man, with such a respect for logic, be deceived by parlor tricks? The answer is that people believe what they want to believe. Sir Arthur had lost a son in World War I. After a medium delivered a message from his son, Sir Arthur desperately wanted to believe it was true. The Conan Doyles were both so committed to Spiritualism that Lady Conan Doyle started trying to channel spirits herself.

Harry kept quiet about his doubts when he first met Sir Arthur. He wanted to remain friends with the great author. Apart from Spiritualism, the two men really got along very well. Sir Arthur was fascinated by Harry's illusions and skills. Even later in life, after they stopped speaking to each other,

Sir Arthur still told people he was sure that Harry had psychic abilities. How else could you explain his escapes? Well, of course, Harry could have explained them, but he wasn't about to reveal his secrets that easily.

The two men first met in 1920, and were close friends for almost two years. But in early 1922, because Harry liked Sir Arthur, he agreed to attend a séance with him. It was a big mistake.

The Conan Doyles were staying in New Jersey during Sir Arthur's lecture tour of the United States. The Houdinis were visiting for the weekend, and Sir Arthur suggested that they try something called an automatic-writing séance. This meant that Lady Conan Doyle would go into a trance and try to contact the spirits. Then she would write down anything they "told" her. Sir Arthur thought perhaps they would be able to contact Harry's mother.

Harry was nervous about the séance, but he

agreed to participate. Perhaps there was some part of him that actually hoped he could communicate with Cecilia. He still missed his mother terribly.

Sir Arthur was thrilled with the results of the séance. His wife filled fifteen pages with messages for Harry, expressing Cecilia's love for him and how much she missed him. Sir Arthur thought Harry had to be as convinced as he was. Surely he couldn't deny this kind of evidence.

Harry didn't want to offend Sir Arthur Conan Doyle. He was polite during the séance and didn't say anything about his  suspicions. But afterwards, in his diaries and letters to friends, he openly revealed all his doubts.

For one thing, he said, Lady Conan Doyle had begun the message by drawing a cross at the top of the page. She said this was a typical "sign" showing that the spirit was "good." But Harry did not think his mother, who was Jewish, would ever have drawn a cross. Even more suspicious, the messages were entirely in English—a language Harry's mother had never spoken. Surely if she really wanted to send a message to Harry, she would have written it in German.

Sir Arthur heard about Harry's comments and was outraged. How dare Houdini accuse Sir Arthur's wife of fraud? To be fair, Lady Conan Doyle was probably not trying to trick Houdini. She really might have thought she was receiving messages from Cecilia Weiss. That's how much  she believed in Spiritualism and in her own connection to the spirit world.

Harry and Sir Arthur started writing angry

letters to each other in April of 1922. The argument quickly moved into the public eye. Newspapers loved the idea of two famous figures quarreling over such a hot issue. They published articles each of them wrote defending his position. On this issue, the two men would always disagree—and it destroyed their friendship.

In the next couple of years, Harry dedicated a great deal of his time to exposing fake mediums and debunking Spiritualists. He even wrote a couple of books about Spiritualism, including *A Magician Among the Spirits*, published in 1924. He challenged anyone to produce some "spirit

phenomena" that he could not reproduce using a magician's tricks. If someone did convince him, he offered to pay them $10,000. As in the case of his earlier Handcuff Challenge, he never had to pay up.

He also traveled the country performing an act specially designed to show everyone how these "mediums" did their tricks. A lot of séances took place in dark rooms, with everyone in a circle holding hands. Harry showed how the medium could use his or her feet and head to create the sounds and effects people heard and saw in the dark. He showed how "psychics" could easily find out information about people to trick them.

Harry sat in on séances all over the USA. He asked the mediums questions that only his mother could answer, saying that if they could really talk to the dead, they would surely be able to get the answer from her. Sometimes he even disguised himself, since a lot of mediums refused to perform a séance with Houdini in the room.

It is possible that Harry really wanted to find a true medium. He would have given anything to be able to speak to his mother just once more. If he had found anyone who convinced him, he said he was willing to admit it. But Harry thought it was terrible to make people, who were often heartbroken and vulnerable, pay for lies and deception. Exposing these frauds was another way Harry felt he was helping people.

Chapter 11
So You Want to Be Remembered Forever

A lot of people think that Harry died during one of his difficult escapes. In fact, there is a movie about his life (mostly fictional), made in 1953, called *Houdini*, in which he drowns during one of his daredevil stunts. His escapes certainly were dangerous and could have caused his death. But that's not what happened.

On the morning of October 22, 1926, Harry was at McGill University in Montreal, Canada. A few days earlier, he had fractured his ankle during an escape. Houdini was limping, tired, and under stress because Bess was suffering from food poisoning. But no matter how bad he felt, nothing would stop him from performing.

Harry was relaxing in his dressing room, having his portrait drawn, when a student from the university knocked and came in. He started asking Harry questions about himself—about his life and beliefs, and, of course, his tricks. Harry was friendly, even though he was tired.

At one point, the student said, "Is it true, Mr. Houdini, that you are so strong, a man could hit you in the stomach, and it wouldn't hurt you?"

Harry was very strong. But more importantly, he knew what to do with his muscles so that he wouldn't get hurt when somebody hit him. It took a moment of preparation and tightening his stomach. So when the student asked if he could try hitting him, Harry said sure. Unfortunately, Harry wasn't really paying attention. Before he had a chance to prepare himself, the visitor started punching him really hard in the stomach.

"Hey, stop that!" the other people in the room gasped. "Are you insane?"

Harry raised his hand, and the student stopped. "That will do," said Harry weakly.

Harry was in a lot of pain. What he didn't know was that the man had accidentally ruptured Harry's appendix. Harry was in serious danger. But he still refused to cancel his shows. He was Harry Houdini. He wasn't going to let a little stomach pain keep him down.

Harry performed his last show in Detroit on

the night of October 24, and then collapsed. Bess insisted on taking him to the hospital, and on October 25 the doctors removed his appendix. Sadly, it was too late for Harry. He had developed a very bad infection from the injury. Harry fought to stay alive for several more days. Finally, he told his brother, Theo, "I'm tired of fighting . . . I can't fight any more." Those were his last words.

Harry died on Halloween—October 31, 1926. He was fifty-two years old. After a huge funeral attended by thousands of people, Harry was buried next to his mother in Machpelah Cemetery, in the New York City borough of Queens.

For years Bess tried to contact Harry's ghost. He had promised her that if it was at all possible to come back and talk to the living, he would find

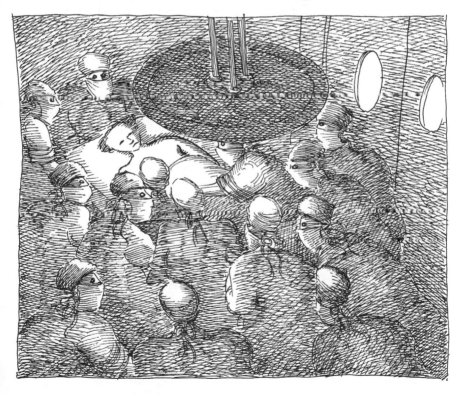

a way to contact her. He even told her a secret message that would let her know it was him for real. But the message never came.

Bess lived for many more years, but she never forgot Harry, and she spent the rest of her life keeping his memory alive.

So what was the magic of Harry Houdini really all about? How did he do his amazing tricks? Well, we do know about some of them. "Metamorphosis" and the "Milk Can Escape" were mostly mechanical—half the trick was in the apparatus he used. Even so, it would be hard (and very dangerous) to duplicate Harry's act. He really could have had a fatal accident doing most of his escapes. But it didn't matter to him. He loved performing, and he loved being famous. He also loved being the only person in the world who could do these tricks.

Harry was born in a time of new discoveries and inventions. He loved the modern world, and his life showed that love—whether it was airplanes, movies, or the triumph of science over Spiritualism. If he lived today, he would probably have been the first performer to have his own website, and he would be trying to figure out ways to escape from a space shuttle.

As a young boy, Harry was one of the millions of people who came to America hoping to make their dreams come true. He spent his life following his dream and put all his energy into everything he did. He showed that anyone can do anything through hard work and believing in himself.

There is a lot of mystery about Harry Houdini even today. People wonder—was there a big secret to his magic that nobody ever knew? Harry liked to make people think so. And some of his tricks are almost impossible to explain. But as Bess always said: it was never really about the tricks. Harry's magic was all in the man, Harry Houdini himself.

TIMELINE OF HOUDINI'S LIFE

1874	Harry (Ehrich Weiss) is born, March 24, in Budapest, Hungary
1875	Harry and his family move to America
1886	Harry runs away from home
1887	Harry moves to New York City with his father
1891	Harry reads *The Memoirs of Robert-Houdin* and is inspired to become a magician
1892	Harry's father, Rabbi Mayer Samuel Weiss, dies on October 5
1893	Harry and his brother Theo perform at the World's Fair in Chicago
1894	Harry meets and marries Beatrice (Bess) Raymond
1899	Harry is discovered by Martin Beck and starts performing in vaudeville houses
1900	Harry and Bess sail to England for European tour
1902	Harry is challenged by William Hodgson in England
1905	Harry and Bess return to America
1908	Harry's milk can trick premieres
1910	Harry becomes the first person to fly an airplane in Australia
1913	Harry's mother, Cecilia Weiss, dies on July 17
1919	Harry performs the Vanishing Elephant trick in New York City
	Harry's first movie, *The Master Mystery*, opens
1922	Harry attends the séance that ends his friendship with Sir Arthur Conan Doyle
1923	Harry's book *A Magician Among the Spirits* is published
1926	Harry dies on October 31

TIMELINE OF THE WORLD

First exhibit of Impressionist paintings is held in Paris — **1874**

Albert Einstein is born — **1875**

The Statue of Liberty is dedicated — **1886**

Sir Arthur Conan Doyle publishes the first Sherlock Holmes story — **1887**

Basketball is invented in Massachusetts — **1891**

Ellis Island opens in New York harbor — **1892**

New Zealand becomes the first country in the world that allows women to vote — **1893**

Rudyard Kipling publishes *The Jungle Book* — **1894**

The Brooklyn Children's Museum opens as the world's first children's museum — **1899**

Dr. Sigmund Freud publishes *The Interpretation of Dreams* — **1900**

First *Tyrannosaurus rex* fossil is discovered
Beatrix Potter publishes the first Peter Rabbit story — **1902**

The New York City subway opens — **1904**

Henry Ford develops the first Model T automobile and sells it for $850 — **1908**

Boy Scouts of America is incorporated — **1910**

First crossword puzzle appears in NY *World* newspaper — **1913**

Lincoln Memorial is dedicated
King Tutankhamen's tomb is discovered — **1922**

Rin-Tin-Tin becomes the first dog movie star — **1923**

Annie Oakley dies — **1926**